What's Heaven?

Written by

Maria Shriver

Illustrated by Sandra Speidel

Golden Books

NEW YORK

Acknowledgments

First, I am very grateful to my daughters, Katherine and Christina,
for asking the questions that led to this book and for helping me to answer them.
I would also like to thank Jan Miller, Bob Asahina, Julia Paige, Ellen Jacob, Cassie Jones,
and Teri Hess. They all provided great insight and kept me focused.
I thank them from the bottom of my heart. And to Sandra Speidel: your illustrations
brought *What's Heaven?* to life. Thank you for believing in this book.

Golden Books®

888 Seventh Avenue
New York, NY 10106

Text Copyright © 1999 by Maria Shriver
Illustrations © 1999 by Sandra Speidel
All rights reserved, including the right of reproduction in whole or in part in any form.
Golden Books® and colophon are trademarks of Golden Books Publishing Co., Inc.

Designed by Ellen Jacob

Manufactured in the United States of America

10 9 8 7

Library of Congress Cataloging-in-Publication Data

Shriver, Maria
    What's heaven? / written by Maria Shriver ; illustrated by Sandra Speidel.
        p.   cm.
    Summary: After her great-grandmother's death, a young girl learns about heaven by asking her mother all kinds of questions.
    ISBN 0-307-44043-5 (alk. paper)
    [1. Heaven—Fiction. 2. Death—Fiction. 3. Great-grandmothers—Fiction.] I. Speidel, Sandra, ill. II. Title.
PZ7.S559173Wh 1999
[E]—dc21
                                           98-49837
                                               CIP
                                                AC

For my children, Katherine, Christina, Patrick, and Christopher.
You are the joy of my life. I love you all deeply. For my
wonderful husband, Arnold, who pushes me to pursue my dreams.
For my parents, Eunice and Sargent Shriver, who always told me
that I could do and be anything I wanted. And for my grandmother,
Rose Fitzgerald Kennedy, whose life inspired me and whose
death brought out these questions. I will always be grateful for
your life, your love, and your wisdom.

—XOXO Maria

For my mother, Lily Ann Speidel.

—S. S.

Once upon a time there was a little girl named Kate. She was the kind of girl whose beautiful eyes sparkled when she talked. Her long brown hair framed her face. Kate loved to ask questions. She wanted to learn about everything. Every time she got an answer, she'd ask another question. ✾ One day Kate came home from school. She saw that her mom was very sad. ✾ Kate asked, "Mommy, why are you so sad?" ✾ Her mom looked at her and said, "My grandma, your great-grandma, has died and gone to Heaven. ✾ Kate thought about this for a moment. Then she asked, "Heaven? What's heaven?"

"Heaven," said Kate's mom, "Is a beautiful place up in the sky, where no one is sick, where no one is mean or unhappy. It's a place beyond the moon, the stars, and the clouds. Heaven is where you go when you die."   "Oh," Kate said. "That's where our dog Shamrock went when she died, and Karen's cat and Bobby's bird?"   Kate's mom nodded. "Do you remember what you felt like when Shamrock died? You were very sad because you were going to miss her. It's kind of the same feeling when a person you love dies," said Mommy. "It hurts deep inside, because you realize that you will never see them again. I cried a lot this morning when I heard my grandma had died. I cried because I will miss her. But I believe Great-grandma is safe in Heaven, so that makes the pain a little less."

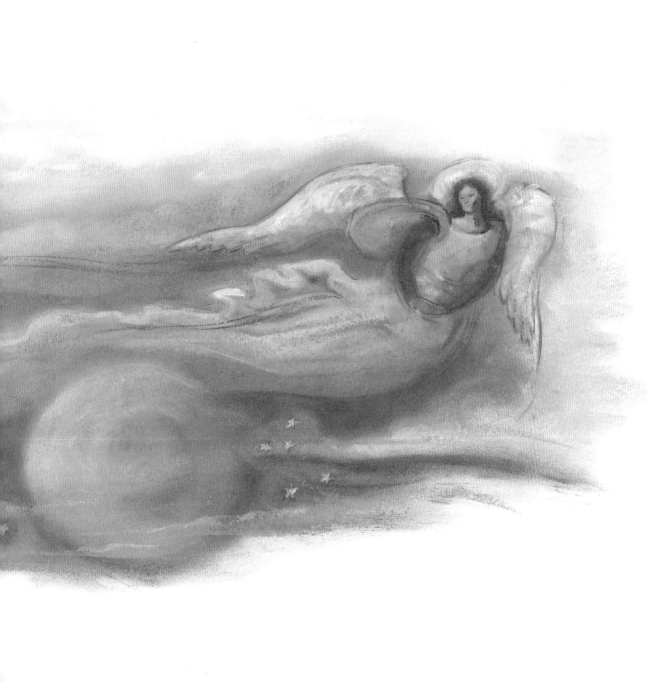

"Is Great-grandma in the same heaven as Shamrock, or do they have a separate heaven for animals and people?" Kate asked. ❧ Before Kate's mom could answer, Kate answered the question herself. "I think they have an animal heaven and a people heaven, and there's a small white fence that separates them. During the day the people and the animals can play together if they want, but at night the animals have to stay in the animal heaven and the people have to stay in the people heaven."

Kate went to her room and grabbed her doll. She walked outside and sat down on the front porch step. She looked straight up at the sky, squinting her eyes really hard. Just then her mom walked out and asked what she was doing. ❧ Kate asked, "If Heaven's in the sky, how come I can't see it?" ❧ Kate's mom sat down next to her and thought for a moment. "Heaven isn't a place that you can see," she explained. "It's somewhere you believe in. I imagine it's a beautiful place where you can sit on soft clouds and talk to other people who are there. At night you can sit next to the stars, which are the brightest of anywhere in the universe. Everyone there is happy to be in such a peaceful place where God will love them forever."

Kate put her finger on her chin and tapped it a couple of times. "I wonder if they wear clothes in Heaven? I bet they wear really pretty flowing clothes like angels." ✎ "You know, Kate, I never thought about that. I bet you're right," said Kate's mom. ✎ "So everyone gets to go to Heaven?" Kate asked. ✎ Her mom replied, "I believe that if you're good throughout your life, then you get to go to Heaven. Some people believe in different kinds of heaven and have different names for it." ✎ Kate was silent for a few minutes. Then she asked, "Mommy, how do you get to Heaven?" ✎ "Well," said her mom, "when your life is finished here on earth, God sends angels down to take you up to Heaven to be with him." ✎ "Do the angels just take you through the ceiling and through the sky?" asked Kate.

Her mom said, "You know, Kate, there are lots of things we don't know about Heaven, but I think that when a person dies, the angels come and take the soul, and leave the body here." ✑ "The soul?" Kate's eyebrows came together in a worried line over her nose. ✑ Her mom said, "Close your eyes. Tell me what you think of when you remember Shamrock." ✑ "I remember that she liked to lick my face and liked to play a lot," Kate answered. ✑ Kate's mom explained, "Shamrock's soul is made up of all the things we can't see, like being friendly and playful. And it's the same with a person. When I close my eyes and think about your great-grandma, I remember that she was kind, loving, and very giving to me. Do you remember how much she loved to spend time with you and listen to your stories? All those things are her soul."

Kate, her mom and dad, her baby brother, Mark, and her four-year-old sister, Emma, then left for Grandma's house. During the drive, Kate thought about all her mother had told her. ✎ When Kate arrived at Grandma's house, many of her cousins were playing outside in the yard. Kate jumped out of the car and hugged and said hello to her family. ✎ Kate's oldest cousin was Bobby. He was eight and knew the answer to every question that Kate asked. Kate couldn't wait to tell Bobby about Heaven.

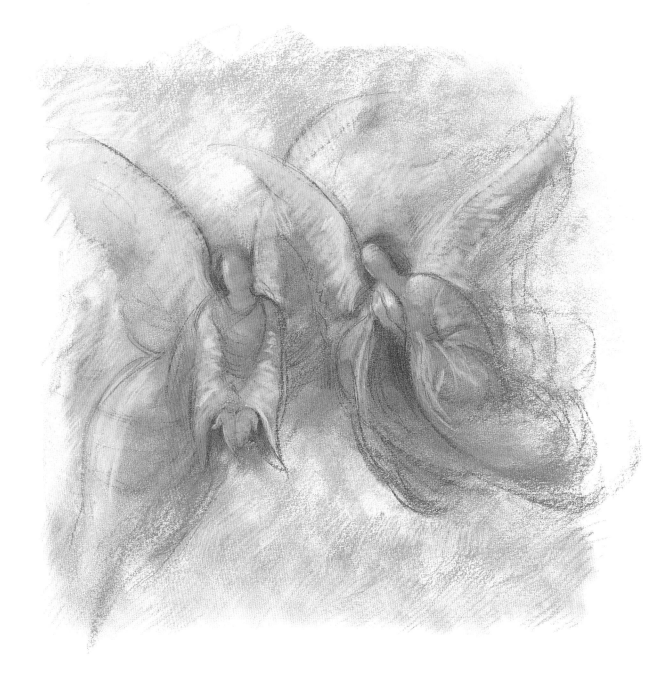

Kate said to Bobby, "Do you know that Great-grandma is in Heaven with our dog, Shamrock?" ❧ "Yes," he answered. "That's why we're all here. We're going to her funeral." ❧ **"What's a funeral?"** asked Kate. ❧ Bobby sat next to Kate on the swingset. As they swung back and forth, Bobby explained, "Great-grandma is going to be put in a wooden box and buried in the ground." ❧ Kate made a face. "They're going to put Great-grandma in a box in the ground?" ❧ "Yup," answered Bobby. "I know that because we buried my bird in a cereal box in our back yard. Lots of my friends have buried their animals when they died." ❧ "I wonder if they did that to Shamrock," said Kate. ❧ "Some people do and some don't. Everyone does it differently," said Bobby.

Ding, dong. Ding, dong. Dinner was ready. Kate and her cousins ran from all directions toward the house. It was time to wash their hands and change their dirty clothes. ❧ Kate put on the pretty dress that her mother had brought her to wear. She grabbed her brush and asked her mom to do her hair. ❧ As her mom combed out the tangles, Kate started asking more questions. "Bobby told me we are going to a funeral where we are going to bury Great-grandma in a box. Why are we going to do that? Will it hurt Great-grandma? How will she breathe in the box? What if she wants to get out?"

Her mom stopped brushing Kate's hair and turned her toward her.

"Great-grandma's body is in the wooden box, but remember, her soul—

all the things that made her a wonderful person—has already been

taken up to Heaven by the angels. Great-grandma's soul doesn't need

to breathe. What's really important for you to remember is that you

shouldn't worry about anybody after they die. They are going to a

beautiful place where they will be happy forever." ❧ "So I guess if

you go up to Heaven, you can't come back. Is that right?" Kate asked.

❧ "That's right, Kate. You go to Heaven when

your life here on earth is over. But no one

who goes to Heaven is forgotten. Their friends and family always

remember them. So, in a way, they live on in all of us."

Kate asked, "So Great-grandma is alive in you?" ❧ "Yes," Kate's mom

said. "Everything she ever taught me is alive in me. She taught me that

it is really important to love my family, to treat others with respect,

and to be able to laugh a lot. Most important, she taught

me to believe in myself." ❧ "Oh," said

Kate. "Those are the same things you always tell me. Now I know

they came from Great-grandma to Grandma to you to me. So

Great-grandma is alive in me, too!"

The next day, Kate, her mom and dad, some of her cousins, and the rest of the grown-ups went to Great-grandma's funeral. Some people cried, some hugged each other, and some were very quiet. "Everyone has their own way," explained Mom. ❧ After the funeral, they drove back to Grandma's house. As they got out of the car, Kate asked, "Why did Great-grandma look so different? She didn't look like I remembered her." ❧ Kate's mom told her, "Remember, that's because only her body was buried today. Her life, her soul, all the things we loved best about her have already been taken to Heaven. When you think of Great-Grandma, remember how she loved to tell you stories about her life as a young girl in Boston. Remember how she played the piano and sang to you. Remember the walks you took with her, and the wisdom she passed on to you. Think of these things when you think of Great-grandma."

Kate's mother's eyes filled with tears. "You know, Mommy," said Kate, "I don't think you should be sad." ❧ "Kate, it's okay to be sad when someone dies," her mother told her. "It's okay to cry. I'll miss my Grandma. I'll miss being able to talk to her and laugh with her. I'll miss her love and support. That's why I'm sad." ❧ "But Mom," Kate said, "Great-grandma is in Heaven. She doesn't have to be sick in a bed anymore. She can play games and go to parties. She's in a safe place, with the stars, with God and the angels and Shamrock. She is watching over us from up there. I just know it." ❧ "You're right, Kate," said her mom. "It's hard to say goodbye to someone you love, but it's also important to know that the sadness won't last forever. And it does make me feel better knowing that she has gone to a place as wonderful as Heaven."

Kate smiled, kissed her mom, and ran off to play. As she did she looked up toward Heaven and said, "Great-grandma, I know you are up there, and if you can hear me, I want you to know that even though you are no longer here, your spirit will always be alive in me."